# WHEN CALL THE PEOPLE

Abhijit Naskar is the twenty-first century Neuroscientist whose contributions in Cognitive and Behavioral Neuroscience have helped the world tackle the issues of mental illness, prejudice, hate, extremism, discrimination and segregation more effectively. As an untiring advocate of mental health and universal acceptance, he became a beloved best-selling author all over the world with his very first book "The Art of Neuroscience in Everything". With his pioneering ventures into the Neuropsychology of beliefs and biases, he has hugely contributed in the eradication of religious and cultural differences in our world, for which he is popularly hailed as a humanitarian neuroscientist, who takes the human civilization in the path of sweet general harmony.

# WHEN CALL
## *the*
# PEOPLE

*My World*
*My Responsibility*

ABHIJIT NASKAR

Also by Abhijit Naskar

The Art of Neuroscience in Everything
Your Own Neuron: A Tour of Your Psychic Brain
The God Parasite: Revelation of Neuroscience
The Spirituality Engine
Love Sutra: The Neuroscientific Manual of Love
Homo: A Brief History of Consciousness
Neurosutra: The Abhijit Naskar Collection
Autobiography of God: Biopsy of A Cognitive Reality
Biopsy of Religions: Neuroanalysis towards Universal
Tolerance
Prescription: Treating India's Soul
What is Mind?
In Search of Divinity: Journey to The Kingdom of Conscience
Love, God & Neurons: Memoir of a scientist who found
himself by getting lost
The Islamophobic Civilization: Voyage of Acceptance
Neurons of Jesus: Mind of A Teacher, Spouse & Thinker
Neurons, Oxygen & Nanak
The Education Decree
Principia Humanitas
The Krishna Cancer
Rowdy Buddha: The First Sapiens
We Are All Black: A Treatise on Racism
The Bengal Tigress: A Treatise on Gender Equality
Either Civilized or Phobic: A Treatise on Homosexuality
Wise Mating: A Treatise on Monogamy
Illusion of Religion: A Treatise on Religious
Fundamentalism
The Film Testament
Human Making is Our Mission: A Treatise on Parenting
I Am The Thread: My Mission
7 Billion Gods: Humans Above All
Lord is My Sheep: Gospel of Human
Morality Absolute
A Push in Perception
Let The Poor Be Your God
Conscience over Nonsense
Saint of The Sapiens
Time to Save Medicine
Fabric of Humanity

Build Bridges not Walls: In the name of Americana
The Constitution of The United Peoples of Earth
Lives to Serve Before I Sleep
When Humans Unite: Making A World Without Borders
All For Acceptance
Monk Meets World
Mission Reality
Citizens of Peace: Beyond The Savagery of Sovereignty
Operation Justice: To Make A Society That Needs No Law
See No Gender
The Gospel of Technology
Every Generation Needs Caretakers: The Gospel of
Patriotism
Aşkanjali: The Sufi Sermon
Mad About Humans: World Maker's Almanac

# DEDICATION

*Madiba*

# CONTENTS

# 1. Preamble

Many people have asked me, where was I born. The answer to this question is not as straight-forward as you may assume. My body was born in a little suburban town on the outskirts of Calcutta, India. But the idea which you know as Naskar had its birth in not one but many places, and that too across the dimension of time. The first foundation stone of that idea was born on the eastern bank of the Hooghly River in India - then one part was born in Chicago - one in Yasnaya Polyana, Russia - one in Cappadocia, Turkey - and one in Pernik, Bulgaria – in that precise order.

I am not a person, I am the antidote to disharmony, born through centuries of mental expeditions in the path of global unification. Hence, I have no one nationality, even though you may find one on my passport. The nationality written on my passport has nothing to do with the nationality written on my heart. Content of my passport are the requirements of governmental operations outside my mind. They don't define the operations inside my mind - nor do they, nay, can they define the content of my mind - and above all they are absolutely powerless in defining the idea called Naskar.

I don't exist you see - I am just a sentience that lives only in people's minds and will keep on living that way forever. So you can exterminate my body, but you can never erase me from the psyche of humankind. When one Naskar dies, a thousand Naskars will rise up to take the place. They will stand up wherever there is bigotry, they will stand up wherever there is discrimination, they will stand up wherever there are injustice and inequality, they will stand up wherever there are oppression, segregation and crisis.

Naskar is not an entity, Naskar is a revolution - Naskar is an evolution - an evolution from segregation to inclusion - an evolution from divisiveness to unity - an evolution from nationality to humanity. And you can kill a person, but there is no power in the world that can impede the force of evolution - the force of nature.

2.  Take My Life (The Sonnet)

## Take My Life (The Sonnet)

Take my life if you want,
But nothing can take my sight away.
Take my breath if you want,
But nothing can take my might away.
Take my feet if you want,
But nothing can take my journey away.
Take my arms if you want,
But nothing can take my touch away.
Take my tongue if you want,
But nothing can take my voice away.
Take my bones if you want,
But nothing can take my will away.
You can erase me from earth if you so
desire,
But you can't stop my ideas from spreading
like wildfire.

# 3.  Rise I Will (The Sonnet)

## Rise I Will (The Sonnet)

Every time there is darkness most foul,
I will burn to bring light, sight and might.
Every time there is misery unbound,
I will churn my soul to outpour delight.
Every time the horizon turns gloomy,
I will rush to the aid as a sentient soldier.
Every time the world is infected,
I will walk the alleys as a living sanitizer.
Every time there is savagery on the rise,
I will be the beacon of human alliance.
Every time bigotry overpowers the minds,
I'll be the call to resuscitate fallen
conscience.
I am not a person but a sentience beyond
time.
Rise I will always in crisis to fortify my
humankind.

# 4. The Maker (Sonnet)

**The Maker (Sonnet)**

Step by step we'll reach the mountaintop,
We'll build roads penetrating impediments.
Bit by bit we'll trash our conformities,
We'll erect civilization upon reason and
sentiments.
Day and night we'll stand tall in service,
Through storm, rain, heat and gloom.
There's no time for selfishness,
Being selfish would bring universal doom.
Sanity is in giving and caring,
It's in every act of collective concern.
Because if you care only for the self,
Deserting your children your neighbors
will run.
The world is our home and we must be its
caretaker.
Comfort is luxury, it's time we rise as the
maker.

# 5.  When Darkness Invades

Catastrophe reveals character - it reveals the flames of light more vividly. The darkest night reveals the brightest light. And right now we are facing such night - and we have two choices, either submit to the darkness or be the light that eliminates the darkness. Even the most stubborn darkness fades away in front of one tiny flame.

A flame doesn't make efforts to eliminate the darkness around, all it does is being itself, and the darkness around it disappears on its own. Here, terms like safety and security have no bearing whatsoever. A candle is safest when not burning, but such an existence doesn't serve its purpose. A candle is alive only when it's burning. Be the candle, burn yourself and the darkness will fade away on its own.

Light in the world has never and will never come from outside - it must come from the inside - it must come from you, for you, my friend - you the plain ordinary everyday human - you the being of conscience and character, are the only light - the only hope - the only salvation to the disease-stricken world of ours.

No matter how life-threatening a virus is, modern medicine in the hands of caring humans comes up with a vaccine sooner or later, but while it is engaged in the development of the vaccine, countless humans are suffering in the meantime, and during that time of hopelessness and helplessness the only vaccine that can relieve their devastation is you.

Vaccines can prepare us for a bodily disease, but no vaccine can prepare us for a societal disease - the only treatment for societal disease is human action. Human irresponsibility does more harm to a society than any virus. So, awaken your vigor and shred the irresponsibility that has been imposed on you by your society in the name of practicality.

Remember, the savior is already here - it's you, it's me, it's each one of us. Savior art thou and thy will be done. We humans are the ultimate vaccine to this disease-stricken society. The integrity of the fabric of society hangs on a thin thread - that is, your sense of responsibility. So long as you the individual feel responsible - feel accountable, for the troubles of your society, the fabric of the society will remain intact, but the moment your responsibility disappears, the society will crumble to ashes.

# 6.  When The Journey Begins

When the 3 pound lump of jelly on top of your shoulders decides to solve an issue of the society, there is no power in any authority that can stop it from doing so. So, once you choose to serve, nothing can stop you - once you choose to lift others, nothing can stop you - once you choose to revolutionize your society, nothing can stop you.

Service is your story - sacrifice is your story - and it'll be uttered for eons, so long as there is a beating heart in even one human. Even after all traces of your physical existence have withered away, your story will be uttered with utmost reverence from lips to lips - your story will never fade away so long as there is a human who sheds a tear in joy and sorrow.

And every single drop of tear that a person sheds in joy because of your story, and every single drop of tear that gets wiped off by your story, will be the greatest wealth that you could ever receive. Your story will stand among the humans as that of a saint. What do you need to do for that to happen you ask! Burn so bright that the sky falls short for your light. Burn for others even if it means putting yourself in harm's way and your story will go on forever with no end.

Feel the breath surge through your lungs like a flood at the sight of those in misery. Once you feel, that's when your real journey will start. And every step that you take in that journey will be chiseled upon the heart of humanity never to wear off. Every step counts - no matter how little you think of it to be. Mother Nature makes such apparently little and insignificant steps every step of the way and over time those very assumedly insignificant steps cause the rise of the most significant evolutionary marvels in the history of life.

So, significant or not, take the first step and make it be followed by another and that with another and so on. And in time, your very journey will become the cause of an evolutionary change for our entire species. Your journey has the potential to carve the path on which our humankind is to walk. Hence, your journey is not just your journey, it's our journey.

Now here I am not talking about those regular copycat journeys that take place in billions, I am talking about those rare original journeys that determine the very fate of our species - the journey of Nikola Tesla - the journey of MLK - the journey of Charles Darwin - the journey of Marie Curie - the journey of Abhijit Naskar - and the journey of so many more. The quantity of these journeys is not that high – in fact, compared to the entire population it's minuscule, yet this apparently minuscule number of journeys determines the very path of an entire species. No step too tiny, no act too futile. Every bit of it counts.

Bit by bit dreams take flight - bit by bit ideas take flight - bit by bit progress takes flight. Remember, the greatest revolutions have their beginning in one tiny step - in one tiny decision - in one tiny action. So, start small and keep walking, and slowly but surely you will reach the mountaintop. The destination manifests through the one who gives their life to the journey.

For the humankind to be free from prejudices - from hatred - from discrimination - from injustice all over the world, a handful of individuals must sacrifice everything - and I mean everything - everyday joy - everyday pleasures - without this sacrifice the torch of liberty - the torch of progress - the torch of human unification - the torch of human acceptance - will go dark.

Darkness is a natural state of the world. Without the presence of light, all we'll have is darkness. You don't have to make efforts to bring darkness, but a few individuals - a few conscientious, courageous bravehearts - a few lionhearts must sacrifice everything - must turn their very existence into a shining torch of progress - of liberty - of unity, so that the humans all over the world can have a humane society - can have an inclusive society - can have a non-judgmental society.

Only the shallow judge others, those with character know to judge themselves before they judge others. We judge others when we are insecure ourselves - we judge when we are not content with our own life - we judge when we ain't happy for who we are - we judge when we lose our soul in the cacophony of superficiality. Superficiality breeds insecurity, simplicity breeds contentment. And once we start living with content, our habit of judging would stop on its own.

The point is, we can't build a non-judgmental society while being judgmental ourselves. And as long as the society is judgmental it'll only create more and more insecure, egotistical snobs. Such a society never allows the children to nourish and strengthen their human side, instead it turns them into mean, competitive machines. And machines may look good in a synthetic society, but not in an organic society.

An organic society is raised on the foundation of emotions - on the foundation of sentiments - on the foundation of humanness. In this humanness reason is also a fundamental element, but reason must not be confused with judgment or cynicism. Reason is driven by curiosity, whereas cynicism is driven by bigotry. Hence, cynicism doesn't bring understanding, reason does, and that understanding enables us to contribute in the making of a humane society.

# 7.  When Character Calls

Now the question that we must ask is, what is a humane society? Because, we must have a plain ordinary everyday realization of what the term humane even means, before we can even visualize a humane society. A humane society is a society where the highest significance is placed upon the human above all external patterns and paradigms - above the paradigms of tradition, culture, faith and so on. But mark you, this doesn't mean that such a society will be devoid of all traditions, cultures, faiths and so on, rather it simply means that, in such a society a human would be first a human then everything else.

In such a society a human helps a human because that's what being human is all about, not because they want to be praised for their help or because they want to covert people by helping. So remember, when someone thanks you for your help, tell them - don't say thanks, instead help others whenever you can and ask them to do the same.

In such a society a human pays attention to character, not to color and creed. Character is above religion - it is above color - it is above intellect - it is above physical attractiveness - it is above social status. The wise is attracted to character, whereas the fools are attracted to everything but character. And the wise is the only one worthy of the title human, because human means sapiens and sapiens means wisdom. So what does that make the fools – animals.

A fool is not one who is unintelligent or illiterate, a fool is one who is unable to look at a person beyond the empty labels. As such, an educated scientist can be a fool - a famous actor can be a fool - an adored sportsperson can be a fool - a popular politician can be a fool. On the other hand, a humble shopkeeper who never attended high school can be a wise one - a construction worker who can barely read and write can be a wise one - a stripper who boldly earns a living by entertaining people can be a wise one. It's not the profession that makes a person wise or fool, it's their character. It's not appearance that makes a creature human, it's character. So, there rises the question - are you a human? It is not my question to you. In fact there is no use of my asking you the question.

The question can do good in the world only if the individuals ask themselves, not to others. So, it is a question for you to ask yourself.

# 8.  When Call The Helpless

What's the point of having blood in your veins, if it doesn't boil at the sight of injustice - what's the point of having electricity in your nerves if it doesn't spark at the sight of misery! Let that blood boil - let that electricity spark - let them saturate every single molecule in your body with the sense of responsibility, only then this society will turn humane. No society is born humane, it must be made humane. No nation is born humane, it must be made humane. No planet is born humane, it must be made humane. Be a rebel - deny all security - and leap to the rescue of others with nothing but a pure indomitable desire to see them happy.

From the Andes to the Himalayas - from the Mississippi to the Ganges - from the Mohave to the Thar - no portion of this planet should be left untouched by your humanizing footsteps - it doesn't mean that you have to travel the world to help all of humanity alone - it only means that you need to break the sleep of silence and stand up as a crutch to the helpless around you, and your actions will cause such a tsunami of humaneness that no shore will remain unsoaked by its warm and rejuvenating torrents.

Even in the face of blazing wildfire, move ahead with the love of the people. In spite of cataclysmic tornadoes, march ahead refusing to step back. Bullets may bring hell down on you - all the artilleries in the world may be charged at you - but never forget o mighty being of conscience, you are the one and only hope for the upliftment of the people - and you have no match in this whole wide world. Bow to people in service and the world will bow to you in veneration.

In the hearts of the helpless stand unbending as the flag of courage. No matter how many deadly weapons come your way, stand on guard as a fierce and fervent soldier protecting the meek and the innocent. This doesn't mean that you won't fall - you will fall, for that's what makes you human, but what makes you an alive human is your will to stand back up after every fall, never to back down. Remember, fall down but never back down.

No fall can incapacitate the sacrificial fervor. So, fall down - fall hard - but then get right back up and start building a new humanizing era. And once you start to strive for people's welfare, paying no heed to your own aching falls, the desolate faces of the forgotten alleys will start to glow with bliss. Become a promise to them my friend sprouting wings of long lost hope. Remember, the real festival is the moment when we wipe the tears off from the faces living in despair. It's no charity mark you. Helping those in need is not charity, it's humanity.

Since when being human became a so-called habit of the rich and privileged! Charity is an illustrious invention of the privileged parts of the world with which they can feel less bad about themselves for being at the fortunate side of the disparities in our society. It's a way for them to feel less guilty, without making any effort.

Charity for the privileged is no different from buying something online that they don't need. It just makes them feel good about themselves. Now here, please go slow, because things are not black and white. I am not saying that all the help that you do by just giving money is futile. Rather what I am pointing out is that it's your intention that determines the true worth of your donation, not the amount. So, ask yourself, is your desire for donating money really any different from say buying the newest model of a smartphone!

Do you want to help, because you want to ease the misery in someone's life, or is it just because you wouldn't mind giving away some money since you have more than enough! Ask yourself, would you give that money, even when you couldn't afford to give it away! Intention is the primary factor, whether you are merely practicing charity or actually practicing humanity. A construction worker who gives a portion of his income to the helpless has more humanity flowing through his veins than a billionaire philanthropist.

And in this context, I give a call to the billionaires today who really want to help people - start by demolishing the salary disparity in your own company and distribute your own salary as well as those of your highest earning employees among all your employees so that the salaries of everybody in your company, starting from the janitor to yourself are the same. And use at least half your company's profit to solve societal issues. Remember, being the richest person on earth won't make you happy, easing the difficulties of others will.

# 9.  When Comes The Crisis

The holy trinity of tackling a crisis is unity, faith and sacrifice. We must stay united as humans above all else, we must have faith in ourselves and in each other and we must sacrifice our self-obsession. Crisis either causes regress or progress depending on the will of the people. It can either break you or make you. And as it happens, the world is going through a period of crisis right now, but whether we look at it as a crisis or as an opportunity to reshape our thinking, depends on us. So use this period as a lesson on how to live life with a concern for all of humankind. Without togetherness no species can live through a catastrophe. In short, without togetherness, there is no species.

Some may wonder, what can they do as mere ordinary humans! To them I say, there is no such thing as an ordinary human. Crisis and willpower can turn even the most ordinary human into the most extraordinary beacon of hope and will. A person without will is not alive in the first place, human or otherwise. Now the question is, do we have will? And, no we are not going into all that philosophical discussion about free will. I am simply asking, do you have will of your own? Don't rush. Take it slow, and think over the question a bit. Let it stir in your mind for a while.

Now let's ask another question - what is will? What is the meaning of will? What is the nature of will? Is it something you eat? Is it something you wear? Is it something you can buy? Is it something that can be handed over to you on a silver platter?

Will is a force of instinct vested in our biology to ensure our survival. The drive for survival, that is, the drive to live, manifests in various forms based on the circumstances. However, in practice, will is pure potential - potential that can fuel your desired endeavors. Where there is will, there is possibility, and where there is possibility, there is scope for upliftment. You have to decide, in which direction you want to take your society. It is all in your hands.

# 10. When Come The Dictators

There is only one way to rule the world, that is - serve the world. You may say, *"I don't want to rule the world, let the politicians do that"*. And though the first part of the statement is rather humble, the second part is horrific. And we don't have the luxury for such humble notions, let alone the horrific one, in our infantile civilization that is, because when justice and humaneness practice indifference, injustice and inhumanity reign over the world. So, either you take control of the world - take control of your own life - or be controlled by a bunch of privileged, egomaniac, misogynist, dictators. So you must stand up at your own free will or you will be kept silent forever.

I'm telling you loud and clear right now - from the very beginning of my journey, I wanted to rule the world - and by rule I do not mean telling people how to live their lives - but by rule I mean, not letting any injustice, inequality, discrimination and bigotry fester in corner of my world - of my homeland earth. The world is my home, it's my hood, and it's under my protection. So before any bigot or segregationist tries to poison it with barbarian fantasies, they'll have to go through me first. Either I'll turn every inhumanity into ashes or I'll become ashes myself while trying. Remember the words from *"Lives To Serve Before I Sleep (The Poem)"*.

*"Lives to serve before I sleep,*
*Cause service is my salvation;*
*Wounds to heal before I sleep,*
*Cause time is wailing for absolution;*
*Bridges to build before I sleep,*
*Cause too many walls are raised already;*
*Peoples to unite before I sleep,*
*Cause civilization is trembling and walking*
*unsteady.*

*Shackles to shatter before I sleep,*
*Cause corruption festers in the stagnant norm;*
*Labels to erase before I sleep,*
*Cause they've only confused our global dorm;*
*Sects to humanize before I sleep,*
*Cause segregation has weakened the human*
*bond;*
*Blades to burn before I sleep,*
*Cause they've turned the world into a bloody*
*pond.*

*Tears to wipe before I sleep,*
*Cause the society is lost in fun;*
*Homes to heal before I sleep,*
*Cause ego has wrecked the nests a ton;*
*Biases to alleviate before I sleep,*
*Cause bigotry has outweighed compassion;*
*Purity to pour before I sleep,*
*Cause all are chasing petty gratification.*

*Spirits to lift before I sleep,*
*Cause the minds are running dry;*
*Gods to build before I sleep,*
*Cause orthodoxy makes humanity cry;*
*Wars to end before I sleep,*
*Cause no life is expendable and puny;*
*Humans to raise before I sleep,*
*Cause where humans act human there reigns*
*harmony."*

Remember, unless we all become rulers of our own life - of our own society, we'll have to face with self-obsessed, bigoted and sickening dictators with orange hairs every step of the way. So, you gotta choose - either be the leader yourself of your life - of your neighborhood - of your society - of your nation - or let a bunch of orangutans make a mess of our beautiful world.

Dictators are no less dangerous than the corona virus. Unless we the people wake up and take charge of our society, every tom, dick and donald will think that grabbing women by their vagina entitles them to not a cell in gitmo, but a nicely furnished room called the oval office inside the white house.

When bigotry, segregation and misogyny occupy the highest office of a nation's government, what do you think happens to the nation - downfall. That's what happens when you close your eyes to disparities - when you turn your back on injustice - when you forget your voice during discrimination. And that only fuels all those inhumanities and multiplies them several folds to haunt not just the peace, sanity and serenity of that specific nation, but of the entire world.

So, shake off your fears and loyalty, and shout aloud with nerves of steel and heart made of thunderbolts - beware all bearers of sectarianism, this is my humankind and I am standing on guard here - so this civilization is off limits - take your business elsewhere, perhaps in the jungle, for that's where you belong.

And every time a crisis arrives at the doorstep of humanity, whether at a neighborhood level or a global level, remind yourself, I am what stands between humanity and the crisis - I am what stands between humanity and injustice - I am what stands between humanity and discrimination and disparities - I am what stands between humanity and dictators. If you want to raise a wall, then be the wall that stands between humanity and inhumanity.

And remember, desperation for recognition doesn't bring greatness, desperation to serve people is what makes a person great. The sign of greatness is humility and the sign of shallowness is narcissism. So, tread very carefully my friend, do not let the instinctual drive of narcissism take over your psyche, for once you do, that's when your downfall begins.

The instinctual drive of narcissism exists in all of us, and it manifests in various situations at various intensity. And once you start enjoying those occasional bursts of narcissism, they'll get dominant over time and slowly begin to take over your personality. And once they are dominant, your brain will literally turn blind towards your narcissism. So, take hold of your narcissism while it's still weak and slowly you will be able to modulate it and fake being a narcissist based on the need of the situation.

Now the question is, what does this fake narcissism even mean? Fake narcissism is the same as fake arrogance, that is, your pretense of arrogance in a situation where utter boldness and confidence are called for. In short, own your instincts as much as possible, don't be owned by them. And you can do that only by practicing awareness of those instincts - awareness of your emotions, thoughts, drives and desires.

Be aware of everything that you are - and I mean everything - your good and your bad - your kind side and your angry side - your gentle side and your rebellious side - your human side and your animal side. And if you are not aware, your inner animal will control your whole life with you in the back seat. And when the individual is run by an animal, the society turns animal. Humaneness begins with you - humanity begins with you. Wake up and be human, and in time the whole world will turn human.

# 11. Break The Walls
## (The Sonnet)

## Break The Walls (The Sonnet)

Let's break the walls my friend,
There ain't no place for segregation no
more.
Let's break the distance my friend,
There ain't no place for pettiness no more.
Let's sing the song of victory,
There ain't no place for savagery no more.
Let's loosen the knots of tradition,
There ain't no time for rigidity no more.
Don't you hear the siren my friend,
Can't you feel the rising sun!
Don't you hear the footsteps of dawn,
It's time to let go of all things barbarian.
Fear not the unknown and unexplored o
friend of mine.
Let's walk together opening doors to one
humankind.

# 12. When Comes Chaos

Above the policies, above the law, above the government, above the constitution, there is a higher principle, that is the principle of individual integrity, without which, no matter how much policies and laws we create, we cannot ensure health, safety and sanity in the society. Without that individual integrity within the hearts of the citizens, no government, constitution, law or policy can ensure order in the society.

Order begins in the heart - in the heart of the individual - in the heart of each one of us - in you, in me, in everyone. Order is not something that can be imposed on us by some government or law enforcement officials - any order which is imposed in such a fashion is bound to fall apart, for it's not born out of responsibility, rather it has its origin in fear. And fear creates insecurity which in turn creates chaos, not order. So, a law that is imposed with the purpose of ensuring order, may give an illusory sense of order in the society for a brief period of time, but in time it only creates more disorder - it only creates more chaos.

For real lasting order to be woven into the fabric of society, the individuals must act orderly out of responsibility, not out of fear of the law. The thread with which to weave the fabric of society is individual responsibility. Now here is the interesting part. We can use a cheap synthetic substitute such as the thread of law in weaving the fabric of society to get instant result, but the society woven from such cheap substitute can never have integrity in its structure, and a society without integrity is bound to fall apart.

An attorney friend of mine said to me recently - *"we must have law, to make sure that people are held accountable"*. To this my reply was - *"are we holding people accountable or are we holding animals accountable, because if people are humans in the first place, they don't need laws"*. However, what my friend mentioned is not wrong, but the point is, though we must have a system of law in the society in order to maintain proper functioning of the society here and now, we must not take it to be the ultimate cure for chaos.

Law is only a temporary fix for chaos, not the cure. The only cure for chaos is individual responsibility. Our focus must always be on stimulating and empowering the sense of responsibility towards the society among the humans from a very early age, not on law and order. This means that we must awaken the sense of responsibility towards our society within us at our own free will and then sow it in the flourishing hearts of the young ones. Uphold society and there will be order, but uphold law and we'll have to chase order for the rest of our life.

# 13. Ain't Good People
## (The Sonnet)

## Ain't Good People (The Sonnet)

Ain't no good people we,
If goodness means blindness.
Ain't no practical folks we,
If practicality means selfishness.
Ain't no sane citizens we,
If sanity means indifference.
Ain't no smart bunch we,
If smartness brings arrogance.
Ain't no articulate minds we,
If articulation means mindless accuracy.
Ain't no civilized society we,
If civilization means hypocrisy.
We are the force capable of mastering a
planet.
Let's live not as machines but conscience
incarnate.

# 14. When Comes Complacency

If we can cause a chaos, we can also cure that chaos, but only if we act promptly and observantly without wasting time on argumentation. The only way to cure a chaos is through observation and action. Observation without action is futile and action without observation is chaos itself. So, both must work hand in hand.

Here is a fact - every field of the society has its place in the proper functioning of the society - science has its place - art has its place - politics has its place - law has its place - economics has its place - sociology has its place, so does every single field that has been ensuring that the wheels of society keep moving. But the point is, from time to time, we must reanalyze our methods in our distinct fields and modify or reshape their purposes based on the need of the time and age.

We simply cannot run the vehicle of society with outdated and rusted wheels. So, we must keep scrutinizing ourselves - our goals - our perspectives - we must scrutinize the very roles of our distinct fields, because complacency would mean the ruin of everything. Only with an active mind, a dedicated heart and valiant footsteps, can we make sure that the vessel of society moves forward and not backward. It's not enough to move, we must make sure that the movement is forward and not backward or in circles.

# 15. When Accountability Calls

Freedom is not the mark of progress - you heard right. Freedom is not the mark of progress, responsibility is. If you really think of it - if you really go deep into it - you'd realize that freedom is not really a new thing - it's been there since we humans were animals in the jungle. In the kingdom of the wild, every animal is free to do whatever they want - whatever their heart desires. So, the question rises - what really has changed?

What changed is that we have developed the capacity to contemplate the implications of our freedom in the lives of others. But the point is, having a certain capacity is not the same as practicing the capacity. And that's precisely what's happening in various parts of the world in reaction to the governmental order of lockdown.

While many people are abiding by the law and staying at home as advised by health experts and government officials, some are revolting against those orders, because they see it as a threat to their freedom. And they are protesting on the streets during a global health crisis, endangering lives, with the slogan *"live free or die"* on their lips.

Those who are resisting quarantine are not advocating for *"live free or die"*, they are advocating *"I must have my freedom even if it means harming others."* Remember, if your freedom comes at the cost of other people's lives, then that's not freedom, it's savagery. Freedom is not freedom that harms others. In short, there is not one but two kinds of freedom, one is animal freedom and the other one is human freedom.

How do we define these two you ask! It's rather simple - freedom without accountability is animal freedom and freedom with accountability is human freedom or civilized freedom. So, it's not merely freedom we should be focusing on, it's civilized freedom.

It's not enough to have freedom, one must know how to practice that freedom. Freedom without accountability does more harm than lack of freedom does. So, be not just free but also accountable. Be accountable of your thoughts - be accountable of your emotions - and above all, be accountable of your behavior.

When animals behave without thinking about the implications of their behavior, they are not to blame, for they lack higher brain capacity to comprehend the implications, but when humans behave recklessly like animals despite possessing the higher brain capacities of comprehension and accountability, they are not just to be blamed, but they lose the right to be called human.

If one is to be called human, one must be accountable. But again, being accountable doesn't simply mean knowing the right from the wrong and yet doing the wrong anyways, being accountable means being aware of the implications and doing the right thing, even if it is uncomfortable. Doing the right thing may be uncomfortable sometimes but it is liberating.

But here is the interesting part, righteousness driven by mere personal desires, is the righteousness of the animal, human righteousness is one which considers the wellbeing of those around. So, be righteous with the consideration for the benefit of others, not just yourself. Wake up my friend, from your sleep of selfishness and hold the torch of community high, for now more than ever light is needed.

Arise my titans and fill the sky with your vigor infinite, pour the seas with your conscience upright, and envelop the lands with your sentience burning bright. You are the cure for all the chaos in the world - you are the nutrition for all the malnutrition in the world - you are the water for all the drought in the world - you are the sun for all the darkness in the world. Remember even the darkest night is no match for the rising sun.

The sun must rise for the darkness to disappear, but if the sun itself spends its whole life sleeping like a log, then the world is bound to live in darkness. So, light the torch. Where is the torch you ask! Look at the mirror. Yes, you are the torch. You are the lamp. You are the sun. Whenever and wherever liberty's in jeopardy, you are to rise with all your might and light, and set freedom free, from the chains of tyranny.

But, now rises another question - does freedom mean that authority is taken out of the hands of external oppressors and is placed in the hands of a bunch of self-obsessed, self-righteous, egotistical, know-it-all bigots and snobs, so that they can say and behave however they like! Let me thicken the context with an excerpt from *"Citizens of Peace"*.

> *"People love to say, everybody is entitled to their opinions. It is one of the greatest fallacies of human habit. Everybody is not entitled to their opinion, not when their opinion advocates for segregation and discrimination. Freedom of speech doesn't mean saying whatever one wants, it means saying what's non-discriminatory, non-prejudicial and nonbarbarian. Bigots may have the right to say that all Mexicans are drug smugglers, all black and brown people are inferior humans, or all nonmuslims are infidels, inside the narrow bounds of their own house, but they are not entitled to express such opinion, when amidst people, amidst a civilized society. Remember, acceptance of bigotry and discrimination is the same as advocating for bigotry and discrimination."*

Such freedom that makes way for discrimination and bigotry, and basically all sorts of inhumanity, is no freedom, but primitiveness in disguise. Such freedom is no freedom - in fact, it's a degradation of the very term. Let me elaborate.

Earlier, I mentioned freedom is not a new thing, but then we were talking about "freedom" in general, in the context of the broad spectrum of lifeforms on earth, but now we have moved from that context, and we are diving into the humane manifestation of "freedom" - the freedom as we humans of the so-called democratic world have grown accustomed to. Countless lives sacrificed everything so that their future generations could have the freedom that they lacked. And now that most of us have that freedom, we have made a mess of that freedom, by abusing it in the worst way possible. Let me give you an example.

If you make boozed up youngsters with no comprehension of civilization your role model, you will end up with a world outwardly sophisticated yet inwardly broken and empty. Remember, a singer who publicly practices eroticism on stage, is no more empowering than a dog who pees at the corner of the street.

Now, here I am not against such freedom of expression, but when obscenity is taken to be a tool of empowerment, instead of empowering anyone it only harms the society way more deeply than oppression does. Their so-called feminism (not to confuse with real advocacy of gender equality) looks something like this - till now men have been treating women like trash, now it's time for the women to treat men like trash, while acting like trash themselves.

Now comes the question, by disapproving such behavior am I doing injustice to the person? And the answer is - perhaps yes. I am doing injustice to the person, because I am telling her what is right and what is wrong. And I wholeheartedly accept that accusation if it rises, but when the behavior of such a person influences millions of impressionable young minds by demonstrating the absurd extent of what's acceptable in the society, she is essentially discouraging their capacity for self-regulation, so by not speaking up against such behavior I would be doing injustice to the society. Hence, it becomes the duty of every single conscientious human to speak up, not against the person mark you, but against that specific behavior. Especially because, failure of self-regulation leads to an unstable psyche and an unstable psyche leads to an unstable society.

In short, self-regulation is an intricate part of healthy human living, and any act of a popular personality that essentially harms that mechanism is basically an act of inhumanity on its own, regardless of whether that act is practiced under the banner of so-called freedom of expression.

Nobody is just entitled to behave the way they want to, for such attitude suits animals, not humans - humans ought to be accountable - humans ought to comprehend the implications of their behavior in the lives of the people around - in the fabric of the society. Regardless of whether an individual is a celebrity, a president or a regular person, accountability is imperative in every single human who even considers to be considered a human. And with popularity the accountability of an individual only multiplies. The more famous you are, the more responsible you ought to be.

Some may say, it's their life and they can do whatever they want with it. To them I say - I know it's hard for you to accept, but you cannot do whatever you like with your life, not in public anyways. You simply cannot live in a human society and act like an animal. So before behaving in a certain way, ask yourself over and over, what impact will it have in the society.

On the other hand, a behavior which may be considered obscene and socially harmful if performed say on stage at a music concert, can be a completely acceptable norm in a completely different context, such as in pornography, which serves its own genuine purpose in the society.

Porn serves the society under the no-nonsense banner of adult entertainment. There is no hypocrisy involved. You don't see adult performers pretending to be role models or advocates of female empowerment. Yet some of those performers, such as those who publicly stand up against child porn, deserve to be called role models way more than many of the so-called celebrities. Because, there's honesty in their work and they are very much aware of the boundaries of their actions. And that's where the very definition of freedom lies.

Freedom is more about knowing your boundaries than to have no boundaries at all.

And here I am not talking about the boundaries imposed on you by the society, I am talking about the boundaries that you yourself raise as a part of your self-regulation apparatus upon contemplation and consideration for others. These boundaries are essential to maintain the integrity of the fabric of society. Let me give you an example.

When I am engaged in a conversation with a physicist and the person is most enthusiastically explaining the functioning of our universe, I prefer to keep my mouth shut unless requested otherwise by the situation. That's because my expertise is in the functioning of the universe inside the humans, not the universe outside. So, for the conversation to be beneficial and productive for those engaged in the conversation as well as the listeners, one must learn to raise certain boundaries - one must learn to embrace the expertise of others, just like one expects one's own expertise to be embraced by others. And this is only one example on raising one's own boundaries in various aspects of life.

In short, boundaries are not necessarily bad, in fact, a society without boundaries is headed for catastrophe. Freedom and boundaries go hand in hand. These boundaries are not boundaries of oppression mark you, they are boundaries of responsibility - responsibility towards the society - responsibility towards the wellbeing of all.

# 16. Mad Wind (The Sonnet)

## Mad Wind (The Sonnet)

Turn into a mad wind,
And blow away the rigidity.
Now the savagery must end,
To do that we must rise as almighty.
Turn into the monsoon rain,
And wash away all sickness.
Whenever a crisis arrives,
We must step up shredding all weakness.
Turn into a purifying wave,
And smoothen the thorns of argument.
Whenever rises differentiation,
We must become the bridge without bent.
The world is unstable and feeble with
insecurity.
We must be its strength offering our soul as
stability.

# 17. When Calls Life

If you want your life to mean something, don't ask how much you have, ask how much you can give. If you can't be the door, be the window in someone's life. The only way to be truly happy is to be the gateway to somebody's happiness. Until giving becomes your first nature, you'll always be chasing the illusive phantom of happiness. The more you chase happiness, the more it runs away from you, but rush to help someone in need and happiness will run towards you.

Remember, every initiative of yours has the potential to change the world. But the moment you become concerned with models and labels, instead of the issues that torture our society day in, day out, you start wasting your potential more on futile argumentation than on bringing actual genuine solutions in the society.

We must not be concerned with models and labels, we are conscientious practical human beings whose initiatives should be dictated by the demands of the circumstances and not by ideologies and schools of thought. When you pay too much attention to a certain school of thought, you lose sight of reality, and when you lose sight of reality, you lose sight of life.

Nature doesn't follow any specific school of thought, yet it has produced the most vibrant and unique kingdom of life. So, do what works, not what a certain school of thought proposes as the right path. Now here, some people may argue, am I also not a school of thought - am I also not an ideology! And that's a valid question, to which I'll reply with a question.

Is the absence of ideology, an ideology? Some intellectual know-it-alls may most proudly shout, *"yes, the absence of ideology is also an ideology"*. To them I say, let me explain the matter with a plain ordinary everyday example. When you are thirsty, come to me, I'll tell you - your thirst is an illusion, because your lack of water is also a kind of possession of water. Theories and philosophical debates may work inside air-conditioned rooms, but to find solutions to grassroot problems of the society, you must step beyond theories.

Theories may give you comfort - theories may give you a sense of security, but no one theory on its own can give you complete, ready-made solutions to the problems of the society, problems like injustice, inequality, poverty and so on. To solve these problems you must be able to observe the good and bad of all available theories and put to practice what works. And where there is no suitable theory available at your disposal that may work, you must improvise. And whatever you do, never place theories, ideologies and labels above the value of life, for theories and ideologies can be replaced, but not a life.

One human life is a thousand times more valuable than a thousand bibles, qurans, suttas and vedas - one human life is a thousand times more valuable than a thousand doctrines and rituals - one human life is a thousand times more valuable than a thousand theories and schools of thought - one human life is a thousand times more valuable than a thousand religions and ideologies.

Life first, everything else later. Everything is compromisable - every scripture, every religion, every theory, every ideology, every school of thought is compromisable, but not a human life. Noble are those who realize this in their bones, for they have understood, beyond mere knowledge, what it means to be human.

There is a difference between knowledge and understanding. Let me elaborate with an example. Knowledge means having the information that water can quench your thirst, whereas understanding is the experience you have while drinking a glass of water after spending hours in thirst. This understanding can also be termed "wisdom".

To solve the issues of our society, we must give our mindforce and lifeforce to understand those issues, not just to know them and argue over them. Argumentation will get us nowhere, only responsible action will bring us salvation. Whatever you do, do it with responsibility, till you drop dead. Make your life mean something by being one of those unique and rare few threads that keep the fabric of society intact.

Maintaining the integrity of the societal fabric is not just the responsibility of the politicians and civil servants, it's the responsibility of all of us, the politician and the civilian alike. In fact, contrary to the popular belief, more responsibility lies on the regular civilian than on the politician, because a politician can only gain a place of authority by the consent of the people.

However, the unfortunate reality is, people find it easier to blame all their problems on politicians and bureaucrats. For example, recently, I've been talking to a lot of my friends and colleagues in different fields about the implications of the pandemic in their distinct fields, and one thing that I found common in most of them, except for my friends in law and order, is their promptness in blaming the issues of our world on either the politicians or the corporate sector. And in fact, this is a common trait which can be seen in most of the human population, that is, the desire to impose blame on either the politicians or bureaucrats or corporations.

And here I am in no way implying that the politicians, bureaucrats and corporations are completely unblamable, However, the point is, each human on earth is as much to blame for the problems of our society, as the politicians, bureaucrats and corporations are. The world is not run by politicians, bureaucrats and corporations on their own.

I know, some may most intellectually argue otherwise, so, to them I say, politicians, bureaucrats and corporations can run the world only and only if the people allow them to do so. This means that they can only abuse their power, resources and authority, if the people allow them to do so. But if the people stay awake, through rain, storm and snow, and never turn their back on exploitation, no politician, bureaucrat and corporate giant would have the capacity to do as they please with their power. So, it's the people who have the ultimate say in what happens to our world, not a bunch of so-called elites and intellectuals. Remember, life begins where the comprehension of the elites ends.

Life inside a glass castle has no relation to life on the ground. And it's the life on the ground that has sweetness in it, with occasional bitterness. But sweet or not, it's real and novel, whereas everything about the life inside the glass castle is cold and superficial. And a world run by an exclusive club of people living inside these glass castles, is bound to be cold and superficial.

What the world needs right now more than ever is warmth - it needs sentiments - it needs reason yes, but it needs reason that is concerned with the wellbeing of all, and not just of the non-negotiable supremacy of facts - it needs attachment, nobility, humility and an unbending sense of community, that is, a genuine sense of belonging to the people around.

People are not just a bunch of numbers - people are not just a piece of land - people are a symposium of hopes - people are a concert of dreams and a symphony of sentiments. And, the only way to truly build a humane and inclusive society is to lose oneself in acts that benefit the people. Remember, there is no them and us, it's all us.

Differences will always be there, but why does it matter, so long as we stand together! Think about the siblings in a family, they fight with each other all the time, they are always at each other's throats, yet when trouble comes at the doorstep of their family, they all stand one. Likewise, we humans shall always have reasons to fight with each other, but above them all there is even higher reason that binds us together and that is the reason of humanity.

I give you a call today o roaring titan, step across the bounds of your body and turn into a force of nature, and the whole world will become clay in your hands for you to shape it as you see fit. Carve this world with the forces vested in you by Mother Nature. Become so grand and glorious with your unselfish actions that a hundred covid19's will fall short to break the spirit of humanity. Become such a beacon of light and hope that even a hundred catastrophes will fall short to sicken the society.

I have said this before, I'll say it again, adopt a neighborhood, make the problems of that neighborhood your own problems and be the solution yourself, and eventually all catastrophe will turn powerless. Remember, servitude is sanctitude, selfishness is destitute. You don't know life, until you have lived for others.

# BIBLIOGRAPHY

Aristotle. Politics. Penguin; Revised, Reprint edition. (2000)

Aristotle. De Anima (On the Soul). Penguin Random House. 1987

Aristotle. Physics. Kessinger Publishing, 2004

Archer M., (2000), Being Human: The Problem of Agency. Cambridge University Press.

Archer M., (2003), Structure, Agency and the Internal Conversation. Cambridge University Press.

Adolphs R (2003) Cognitive neuroscience of human social behaviour. Nature Rev Neurosci 4: 165–178.

Adolphs R, Tranel D, Damasio AR (2003) Dissociable neural systems for recognizing emotions. Brain Cogn 52: 61–69.

Afton, A. D. (1985). Forced copulation as a reproductive strategy of male lesser scaup: A field test of some predictions. - Behaviour 92, p. 146-167.

Allison T, Puce A, McCarthy G. (2000) Social perception from visual cues: role of the STS region. Trends Cogn Sci 4: 267–278.

Andresen, Jensine, and Robert Forman, eds. Cognitive Models and Spiritual Maps. Bowling Green, Ohio: Imprint Academic, 2000.

Ashbrook, James, and Carol Albright. The Humanizing Brain: Where Religion and Neuroscience Meet. Cleveland, OH: Pilgrim Press, 1997.

Azari, Nina, Janpeter Nickel, Gilbert Wunderlich, Michael Niedeggen, Harald Hefter, Lutz Tellmann, Hans Herzog, Petra Stoerig, Dieter Birnbacher, and Rudiger Seitz. "Neural Correlates of Religious Experience."

European Journal of Neuroscience 13, no. 8 (2001)

Agar, N. (2004). Liberal eugenics: In defence of human enhancement. London: Blackwell Publishing.

Alteheld, N., Roessler, G., Vobig, M., & Walter, R. (2004). The retina implant new approach to a visual prosthesis. Biomedizinische Technik, 49(4), 99–103.

Antal, A., Nitsche, M. A., Kincses, T. Z., Kruse, W., Hoffmann, K. P., & Paulus, W. (2004a). Facilitation of visuo-motor learning by transcranial direct current stimulation of the motor and extrastriate visual areas in humans. European Journal of Neuroscience, 19(10), 2888–2892.

Bhat Z, Kumar, S, Bhat H (2015) In vitro meat production. Challenges and benefits over conventional meat production. J Sci Food Agric 14: 241–248

Bernstein R. J., (1967), John Dewey. New York: Washington Square Press.

Bernstein R.J., (1971), Praxis and Action: Contemporary Philosophies of Human Activity. Philadelphia: University of Pennsylvania Press.

Bernstein R.J., (1976), The Restructuring Social and Political Thought.

Bernstein R.J., (1983), Beyond Relativism and Objectivism: Science, Hermeneutics, and Praxis. Philadelphia: University of Pennsylvania Press.

Bernstein R.J., (1986), Philosophical Profiles. Philadelphia: University of Pennsylvania Press.

Bernstein R.J., (1991), New Constellation. Cambridge: MIT Press.

Barash, D. P. (1977). Sociobiology of rape in mallards (Anas platyrhynchos):

Responses of the mated male. - Science 197, p. 788-789.

Berger, J. (1986). Wild horses of the great basin: Social competition and population size. - The University of Chicago Press, Chicago.

Birkhead, T. R., Johnson, S. D. & Nettleship, D. N. (1985). Extra-pair matings and mate guarding in the common murre Uria aalge. - Anim. Behav. 33, p. 608-619.

Beauregard, Mario, and Vincent Paquette. "Neural Correlates of a Mystical Experience in Carmelite Nuns." Neuroscience Letters 405, no. 3 (2006)

Benson, Herbert. Timeless Healing: The Power and Biology of Belief. New York: Scribner, 1996

Bogen, J.E.(1995a), 'On the neurophysiology of consciousness: Part I. An overview', Consciousness and Cognition, 4.

Bogen, J.E. (1995b), 'On the neurophysiology of consciousness: Part II. Constraining the semantic problem', Consciousness and Cognition, 4.

Bremner, J. D., R. Soufer, et al. (2001). "Gender differences in cognitive and neural correlates of remembrance of emotional words." Psychopharmacol Bull 35 (3).

Brothers, L. (2002). The social brain: A project for integrating primate behavior and neurophysiology in a new domain. In J. T. Cacioppo et al. (Eds.), Foundations in neuroscience. Cambridge, MA: MIT Press.

Buss, D. D. (2003). Evolutionary Psychology: The New Science of Mind, 2nd ed. New York: Allyn & Bacon.

Buss, D. M. (1989). "Conflict between the sexes: Strategic interference and the evocation of anger and upset." J Pers Soc Psychol 56 (5).

Buss, D. M. (1995). "Psychological sex differences. Origins through sexual selection." Am Psychol 50 (3).

Buss, D. M. (2002). "Review: Human Mate Guarding." Neuro Endocrinol Lett 23 (Suppl 4).

Buss, D. M., and D. P. Schmitt (1993). "Sexual strategies theory: An evolutionary perspective on human mating." Psychol Rev 100 (2).

Blakemore SJ, Decety J (2001) From the perception of action to the understanding of intention. Nature Rev Neurosci 2: 561.

Bruce C, Desimone R, Gross CG (1981) Visual properties of neurons in a polysensory area in superior temporal sulcus of the macaque. J Neurophysiol 46: 369–384.

Buccino G, Vogt S, Ritzl A, Fink GR, Zilles K, Freund HJ, Rizzolatti G (2004) Neural circuits underlying imitation of hand actions: an event related fMRI study. Neuron 42: 323–34.

Colapietro V., (1988), "Human Agency: The Habits of Our Being." Southern Journal of Philosophy, XXVI, 2, pp. 153-68.

Colapietro V., (1992), "Purpose, Power, and Agency." The Monist, 75, 4 (October) pp. 423-44.

Colapietro V., (2003), "Signs and their vicissitudes: Meanings in excess of consciousness and functionality." Logica, Dialogica, Ideologica, a cure di Susan Petrilli e Patrizia Calefato (Milano: Mimesis), pp. 221-36.

Colapietro V., (2004a), "C. S. Peirce's Reclamation of Teleology." Nature in American Philosophy, ed. Jean De Groot (Washington, D.C.: Catholic University Press of America), pp. 88-108.

Colapietro V., (2004b), "Portrait of a Historicist: An Alternative Reading of

Peircean Semiotic." Semiotiche, 2/04 [maggio 2004], pp. 49-68.

Colapietro V., (2006), "Engaged Pluralism: Between Alterity and Sociality." The Pragmatic Century: Conversations with Richard J. Bernstein (Albany, NY: SUNY Press), pp. 39-68.

Colapietro V., (2009), "Habit, Competence, and Purpose." Forthcoming in The Transactions of the Charles S. Peirce Society. Calder AJ, Keane J, Manes F, Antoun N, Young AW (2000) Impaired recognition and experience of disgust following brain injury. Nature Neurosci 3: 1077–1078.

Carey DP, Perrett DI, Oram MW (1997) Recognizing, understanding and reproducing actions. In: Jeannerod M, Grafman J (eds) Handbook of neuropsychology. Vol. 11: Action and cognition. Elsevier, Amsterdam.

Carr L, Iacoboni M, Dubeau MC, Mazziotta JC, Lenzi GL (2003) Neural mechanisms of empathy in humans: a relay from neural systems for imitation to limbic areas. Proc Natl Acad Sci USA 100: 5497–5502.

Changeux JP, Ricoeur P (1998) La nature et la règle. Odile Jacob, Paris.

Cochin S, Barthelemy C, Roux S, Martineau J (1999) Observation and execution of movement: similarities demonstrated by quantified electroencephalograpy. Eur J Neurosci 11: 1839– 1842.

Chomsky Noam, (2017) Requiem for the American Dream

Chomsky Noam, (2016) Who Rules the World?

Chomsky Noam, (2010) How the World Works

Churchland, P.S. (1986), Neurophilosophy (Cambridge, MA: The MIT Press).

Churchland, P.S. & Ramachandran, V.S. (1993), 'Filling in: Why Dennett is wrong', in Dennett and His Critics: Demystifying Mind, ed. B. Dahlbom (Oxford: Blackwell Scientific Press).

Churchland, P.S., Ramachandran, V.S. & Sejnowski, T.J. (1994), 'A critique of pure vision', in Large- scale Neuronal Theories of the Brain, ed. C. Koch & J.L. Davis (Cambridge, MA: The MIT Press).

Crick, F. (1994), The Astonishing Hypothesis: The Scientific Search for the Soul (New York: Simon and Schuster).

Crick, F. (1996), 'Visual perception: rivalry and consciousness', Nature, 379.

Crick, F. & Koch, C. (1992), 'The problem of consciousness', Scientific American, 267.

Craig AD (2002) How do you feel? Interoception: the sense of the physiological condition of the body. Nature Rev Neurosci 3: 655–666.

Damasio, A (2003a) Looking for Spinoza. Harcourt Inc. Damasio A (2003b) Feeling of emotion and the self. Ann NY Acad Sci 1001: 253–261.

d'Aquili, Eugene. "Senses of Reality in Science and Religion." Zygon 17, no 4 (1982)

d'Aquili, Eugene. "The Biopsychological Determinants of Religious Ritual Behavior." Zygon 10, no. 1 (1975)

d'Aquili, Eugene. "The Myth-Ritual Complex: A Biogenetic Structural Analysis." Zygon 18, no. 3 (1983) d'Aquili, Eugene, and Andrew Newberg. The Mystical Mind: Probing the Biology of Religious Experience. Minneapolis: Fortress Press, 1999.

Daly DD. 1958. Ictal affect. Am J Psychiatry.

Damasio, A. (1994) Descartes' Error: Emotion, Reason and the Human Brain. New York, Putnams.

Damasio, A. (1999) The Feeling of What Happens: Body, Emotion and the Making of Consciousness. London, Heinemann.

Darwin, C. (1859) On the Origin of Species by Means of Natural Selection. London, Murray.

Darwin, C. (1871) The Descent of Man and Selection in Relation to Sex. London, John Murray.

Darwin, C. (1872) The Expression of the Emotions in Man and Animals. London, John Murray; also published

1965, Chicago, University of Chicago Press.

Dawkins, M.S. (1987) Minding and mattering. In C. Blakemore and S. Greenfield (eds) Mindwaves. Oxford, Blackwell, 151-60.

Dawkins, R. (1976) The Selfish Gene. Oxford, Oxford University Press; a new edition, with additional material, was published in 1989.

Dawkins, R. (1986) The Blind Watchmaker. London, Longman.

Di Pellegrino G, Fadiga L, Fogassi L, Gallese V, Rizzolatti G (1992) Understanding motor events: A neurophysiological study. Exp Brain Res 91: 176–80.

Deikman, A.J. (2000) A functional approach to mysticism. Journal of Consciousness Studies 7(11-12), 75-91.

Delmonte, M.M. (1987) Personality and meditation. In M. West (ed.) The

Psychology of Meditation. Oxford, Clarendon Press, 118-32.

Dennett, D.C. (1987) The Intentional Stance. Cambridge, MA, MIT Press.

Dennett, D.C. (1988) Quining qualia. In A.J. Marcel and E. Bisiach (eds) Consciousness in Contemporary Science. Oxford, Oxford University Press, 42-77.

Dennett, D.C. (1991) Consciousness Explained. Boston, MA, and London, Little, Brown and Co.

Dennett, D.C. (1995a) Darwin's Dangerous Idea. London, Penguin.

Dennett, D.C. (1995b) The unimagined preposterousness of zombies. Journal of Consciousness Studies 2(4), 322-6.

Dennett, D.C. (1995c) Cog: steps towards consciousness in robots. In T. Metzinger (ed.) Conscious Experience. Thorverton, Devon, Imprint Academic, 471-87.

Dennett, D.C. (1995d) The path not taken. Behavioral and Brain Sciences 18, 252-3; commentary on N. Block, On a confusion about a function of consciousness. Behavioral and Brain Sciences 18, 227.

Dennett, D.C. (1996a) Facing backwards on the problem of consciousness. Journal of Consciousness Studies 3(1), 4-6.

Dennett, D.C. (1996b) Kinds of Minds: Towards an Understanding of Consciousness. London, Weidenfeld & Nicolson.

Dennett, D.C. (1997) An exchange with Daniel Dennett. In J. Searle (ed.) The Mystery of Consciousness. New York, New York Review of Books, 115-19.

Dennett, D.C. (1998) The myth of double transduction. In S.R. Hameroff, A.W. Kaszniak and A. C. Scott (eds) Toward a Science of Consciousness: The Second Tucson Discussions and

Debates. Cambridge, MA, MIT Press, 97-107.

Dennett, D.C. (1998b) Brainchildren: Essays on Designing Minds. Cambridge, MA, MIT Press.

Dennett, D.C. (2001) The fantasy of first person science. Debate with D. Chalmers, Northwestern University, Evanston, IL, February 2001.

Dennett, D.C. (2003) Freedom Evolves. New York, Penguin.

Dennett, D.C. and Kinsbourne, M. (1992) Time and the observer: the where and when of consciousness in the brain. Behavioral and Brain Sciences 15, 183-247, including commentaries and authors' responses.

Dewey J., (1911 [1977]), "Epistemological Realism: The Alleged Ubiquity of the Knowledge Relation." Journal of Philosophy, VIII, 20 (September 28, 1911).

Dewhurst, Kenneth, and A. W. Beard. "Sudden Religious Conversions in Temporal Lobe Epilepsy." British Journal of Psychiatry 117 (1970)

Dewhurst K, Beard AW. Sudden religious conversions in temporal lobe epilepsy. 1970 Epilepsy Behav 2003

Devinsky O, Lai G. Spirituality and religion in epilepsy. Epilepsy Behav 2008.

Devinsky, O., Morrell, MJ, Vogt, BA. (1995) 'Contribution of anterior cingulate cortex to behavior', Brain, 118.

Douglas Stone A., Chapter 24, The Indian Comet, in the book Einstein and the Quantum, Princeton University Press, Princeton, New Jersey, 2013.

E. Horvitz, "One Hundred Year Study on Artificial Intelligence: Reflections and Framing," ed: Stanford University, 2014.

Einstein A. (1925). "Quantentheorie des einatomigen idealen Gases". Sitzungsberichte der Preussischen Akademie der Wissenschaften.

Eckhart Meister, Selected Writings

Egidi R., ed. (1999), "Von Wright and 'Dante's Dream': Stages in a Philosophical Pilgrim's Progress", in In Search of a New Humanism: the Philosophy of G.H. von Wright, ed. by R. Egidi, Kluwer, Dordrecht.

Fadiga L, Fogassi L, Pavesi G, Rizzolatti G (1995) Motor facilitation during action observation: a magnetic stimulation study. J Neurophysiol 73: 2608–2611.

Fogassi L, Gallese V, Fadiga L, Rizzolatti G (1998) Neurons responding to the sight of goal directed hand/arm actions in the parietal area PF (7b) of the macaque monkey. Soc Neurosci Abs 24:257.5.

Frith U, Frith CD (2003) Development and neurophysiology of mentalizing. Philos Trans R Soc Lond B Biol Sci 358: 459.

Farah, M.J. (1989), 'The neural basis of mental imagery', Trends in Neurosciences, 10.

Finlay BL, Darlington RB (1995) Linked regularities in the development and evolution of mammalian brains. Science 268.

Freud, S. "The Interpretation of Dreams", 1900

Freud, S. "Selected papers on hysteria and other psychoneuroses" Journal of Nervous and Mental Disease 1909.

Freud, S. "The Origin and Development of Psychoanalysis", 1910

Freud, S. "Psychopathology of everyday life", 1914

Freud, S. "Beyond the Pleasure Principle", 1920

Frith, C.D. & Dolan, R.J. (1997), 'Abnormal beliefs: Delusions and memory', Paper presented at the May, 1997, Harvard Conference on Memory and Belief.

Gay, Volney, ed. Neuroscience and Religion. Plymouth, UK: Lexington Books, 2009.

Gazzaniga, M. S. (1985). The social brain. New York: Basic Books.

Gazzaniga, M.S. (1993), 'Brain mechanisms and conscious experience', Ciba Foundation Symposium, 174.

Geschwind N. "Behavioural changes in temporal lobe epilepsy". Psychol Med. 1979.

Gellhorn, E., Kiely, W.F. "Mystical states of consciousness: neurophysiological and clinical aspects." J Nerv Ment Dis. 1972;154:399-405.

Gilbert SL, Dobyns WB, Lahn BT (2005) Genetic links between brain development and brain evolution. Nat Rev Genet 6.

Gray JA. The Psychology of Fear and Stress. 2nd ed. New York, NY: Cambridge University Press; 1988.

Gloor, P. (1992), 'Amygdala and temporal lobe epilepsy', in The Amygdala: Neurobiological Aspects of Emotion, Memory and Mental Dysfunction, ed J.P. Aggleton (New York: Wiley-Liss).

Greenspan, S. I. and S. G. Shanker (2004). The first idea: How symbols, language, and intelligence evolved from our early primate ancestors to modern humans. Cambridge, MA: Da Capo Press.

Grady, D. (1993), 'The vision thing: Mainly in the brain', Discover, June.

Gallagher HL, Frith CD (2003) Functional imaging of 'theory of mind'. Trends Cogn Sci 7: 77.

Gallese V, Fogassi L, Fadiga L, Rizzolatti G (2002) Action representation and the inferior parietal lobule. In: Prinz W, Hommel B (eds) Attention & Performance XIX. Common mechanisms in perception and action. Oxford University Press, Oxford.

Gallese V, Keysers C, Rizzolatti G (2004) A unifying view of the basis of social cognition. Trends Cogn Sci 8: 396–403.

Gangitano M, Mottaghy FM, Pascual-Leone A (2001) Phase specific modulation of cortical motor output during movement observation. NeuroReport 12: 1489–1492.

Gangitano M, Mottaghy FM, Pascual-Leone A (2004) Modulation of premotor mirror neuron activity during observation of unpredictable grasping movements. Eur J Neurosci 20: 2193– 2202.

Goldman AI, Sripada CS (2004) Simulationist models of face-based emotion recognition. Cognition 94: 193–213.

Grèzes J, Costes N, Decety J (1998) Top-down effect of strategy on the perception of human biological motion: a PET investigation. Cogn Neuropsychol 15: 553–582.

Grèzes J, Armony JL, Rowe J, Passingham RE (2003) Activations related to "mirror" and "canonical" neurones in the human brain: an fMRI study. Neuroimage 18: 928–937.

Gross CG, Rocha-Miranda CE, Bender DB (1972) Visual properties of neurons in the inferotemporal cortex of the macaque. J Neurophysiol 35: 96–111.

Hari R, Forss N, Avikainen S, Kirveskari S, Salenius S, Rizzolatti G

(1998) Activation of human primary motor cortex during action observation: a neuromagnetic study. Proc. Natl Acad Sci USA 95: 15061–15065.

Hardy, G. H. (1940). Ramanujan. Cambridge: Cambridge University Press.

Hall, Daniel, Keith Meador, and Harold Koenig. "Measuring Religiousness in Health Research: Review and Critique." Journal of Religion and Health 47, no. 2 (2008)

Harris, Sam, Jonas Kaplan, Ashley Curiel, Susan Bookheimer, Marco Iacoboni, and Mark Cohen. "The Neural Correlates of Religious and Nonreligious Belief." PLoS One 4, no. 10 (October 1, 2009)

Halgren, E. (1992), 'Emotional neurophysiology of the amygdala within the context of human cognition', in The Amygdala:

Neurobiological Aspects of Emotion, Memory and Mental Dysfunction, ed J.P. Aggleton (New York: Wiley-Liss).

Halligan PW, Fink GR, Marshal JC, Vallar G. 2003. Spatial cognition: evidence from visual neglect. Trends Cogn Sci.

Handbook of Emotions, Edited by Michael Lewis, Jeannette M. Haviland-Jones, and Lisa Feldman Barrett, The Guilford Press; 3rd edition (2010).

Haggard, P., Clark, S. and Kalogeras, ]. (2002) Voluntary action and conscious awareness, Nature Neuroscience 5, 382-5. Haggard, P., Newman, C. and Magno, E. (1999) On the perceived time of voluntary actions. British Journal of Psychology 90, 291-303.

Hameroff, S.R. and Penrose, R. (1996) Conscious events as orchestrated space-time selections. Journal of Consciousness Studies 3(1), 36-53; also reprinted in J. Shear (ed.) (1997)

Explaining Consciousness-The Hard Problem. Cambridge, MA, MIT Press, 177-95.

Hardcastle, V.G. (2000) How to understand theN in NCC. InT. Metzinger (ed.) Neural Correlates of Consciousness. Cambridge, MA, MIT Press, 259-64.

Harding, D.E. (1961) On Having no Head: Zen and the Re-Discovery of the Obvious. London, Buddhist Society.

Hardy, A. (1979) The Spiritual Nature of Man: A Study of Contemporary Religious Experience. Oxford, Clarendon Press.

Hamad, S. (1990) The symbol grounding problem. Physica D 42, 335-46.

Hamad, S. (2001) No easy way out. The Sciences 41(2), 36-42.

Harre, R. and Gillett, G. (1994) The Discursive Mind. Thousand Oaks, CA, Sage.

Haugeland, J. (ed.) (1997) Mind Design II: Philosophy, Psychology, Artificial Intelligence. Cambridge, MA, MIT Press.

Hauser, M.D. (2000) Wild Minds: What Animals Really Think. New York, Henry Holt and Co.; London, Penguin.

Hearne, K. (1990) The Dream Machine. Northants, Aquarian.

Hebb, D.O. (1949) The Organization of Behavior. New York, Wiley.

Helmholtz, H.L.F. von (1856-67) Treatise on Physiological Optics.

Hess, EH (1975) "The role of pupil size in communication," Scientific American, 233(5), 110–12.

Heyes, C.M. (1998) Theory of mind in nonhuman primates. Behavioral and

Brain Sciences 21, 101-48; with commentaries.

Heyes, C.M. and Galef, B.G. (eds) (1996) Social Learning in Animals: The Roots of Culture. San Diego, CA, Academic Press.

Hilgard, E.R. (1986) Divided Consciousness: Multiple Controls in Human Thought and Action. New York, Wiley.

Hocquette JF (2016) Is in vitro meat the

solution for the future? Meat Science 120:

167–176

Hodgson, R. (1891) A case of double consciousness. Proceedings of the Society for Psychical Research 7, 221-58.

Hofstadter, D.R. (1979) Code!, Escher, Bach: An Eternal Golden Braid. London, Penguin.

Hofstadter, D.R. and Dennett, D.C. (eds) (1981) The Mind's I: Fantasies and Reflections on Self and Soul. London, Penguin.

Holland, J. (ed.) (2001) Ecstasy: The Complete Guide: A Comprehensive Look at the Risks and Benefits of MDMA. Rochester, VT, Park Street Press.

Holmes, D.S. (1987) The influence of meditation versus rest on physiological arousal. In M. West (ed.) The Psychology of Meditation. Oxford, Clarendon Press, 81-103.

Holt, J. (1999) Blindsight in debates about qualia. Journal of Consciousness Studies 6(5), 54-71.

Horgan, J. (1994), 'Can science explain consciousness?', Scientific American, 271.

Holloway RL (1996) Evolution of the human brain. In: Lock A, Peters CR (eds) Handbook of human symbolic evolution. Oxford University Press, Oxford

Iacoboni M, Woods RP, Brass M, Bekkering H, Mazziotta JC, Rizzolatti G (1999) Cortical mechanisms of human imitation. Science 286: 2526–2528.

Iacoboni M, Koski LM, Brass M, Bekkering H, Woods RP, Dubeau MC, Mazziotta JC, Rizzolatti G (2001) Reafferent copies of imitated actions in the right superior temporal cortex. Proc Natl Acad Sci USA 98: 13995–13999.

Jeannerod M (1988) The neural and behavioural organization of goal-directed movements. Clarendon Press, Oxford.

Johnson-Frey SH, Maloof FR, Newman-Norlund R, Farrer C, Inati S, Grafton ST (2003) Actions or hand-objects interactions? Human inferior frontal cortex and action observation. Neuron 39: 1053–1058.

Jackson, F. (1982) Epiphenomenal qualia. Philosophical Quarterly 32, 127-36.

James, W. (1890) The Principles of Psychology (2 volumes). London, Macmillan.

James, W. (1902) The Varieties of Religious Experience: A Study in Human Nature. New York and London, Longmans, Green and Co.

Jansen, K. (2001) Ketamine: Dreams and Realities. Sarasota, FL, Multidisciplinary Association for Psychedelic Studies.

Jay, M. (ed.) (1999) Artificial Paradises: A Drugs Reader. London, Penguin.

Jaynes, J. (1976) The Origin of Consciousness in the Breakdown of the Bicameral Mind. New York, Houghton Mifflin.

Johnson, M.K. and Raye, C.L. (1981) Reality monitoring. Psychological Review 88, 67-85.

Kadim I, Mahgoub O, Baqir S et al. (2015) Cultured meat from muscle stem cells: a review of challenges and prospects. J Integr Agr 14: 222–233

Koski L, Iacoboni M, Dubeau MC, Woods RP, Mazziotta JC (2003) Modulation of cortical activity during different imitative behaviors. J Neurophysiol 89: 460–471.

Krolak-Salmon P, Henaff MA, Isnard J, Tallon-Baudry C, Guenot M, Vighetto A, Bertrand O, Mauguiere F (2003) An attention modulated response to disgust in human ventral anterior insula. Ann Neurol 53: 446–453.

Kandel, E. R. In Search of Memory: The Emergence of a New Science of Mind, W. W. Norton & Company (2007).

Kandel E. R. Schwartz JH, Jessel TM. Principles of neural sciences. New York; McGraw Hill, 2000.

Kanizsa, G. (1979), Organization In Vision (New York: Praeger).

Kaloupek DG, Scott JR, Khatami V. Assessment of coping strategies associated with syncope in blood donors. J Psychosom Res. 1985;29:207-214.

Kanwisher, N. (2001) Neural events and perceptual awareness. Cognition 79, 89-113; also reprinted inS. Dehaene (ed.) The Cognitive Neuroscience of Consciousness. Cambridge, MA, MIT Press, 89-113.

Kapleau, Roshi P. (1980) The Three Pillars of Zen: Teaching, Practice, and Enlightenment (revised edn). New York, Doubleday.

Karn, K. and Hayhoe, M. (2000) Memory representations guide

targeting eye movements in a natural task. Visual Cognition 7, 673-703.

Kasamatsu, A. and Hirai, T. (1966) An electroencephalographic study on the Zen meditation (zazen). Folia Psychiatrica et Neurologica Japonica 20, 315-36.

Kaiserman-Abramof, I. R., Graybiel, A. M., & Nauta, W. J. (1980). The thalamic projection to cortical area 17 in a congenitally anophthalmic mouse strain. Neuroscience, 5, 41–52.

Kanold, P. O., Kara, P., Reid, R. C., & Shatz, C. J. (2003). Role of subplate neurons in functional maturation of visual cortical columns. Science, 301, 521–525.

Kennedy, H., & Dehay, C. (1988). Functional implications of the anatomical organization of the callosal projections of visual areas V1 and V2 in the macaque monkey. Behav. Brain Res., 29, 225–236.

Kentridge, R.W. and Heywood, C.A. (1999) The status of blindsight. Journal of Consciousness Studies 6(5), 3-11.

Kihlstrom, J.F. (1996) Perception without awareness of what is perceived, learning without awareness of what is learned. In M. Velmans (ed.) The Science of Consciousness. London, Routledge, 23-46.

Kollerstrom, N. (1999) The path of Halley's comet, and Newton's late apprehension of the law of gravity. Annals of Science 56, 331-56.

Kosslyn, S.M. (1980) Image and Mind. Cambridge, MA, Harvard University Press.

Kosslyn, S.M. (1988) Aspects of a cognitive neuroscience of mental imagery. Science 240, 1621-6.

Kinsbourne, M. (1995), 'The intralaminar thalamic nucleii', Consciousness and Cognition, 4.

Kjaer, Troels, Camilla Bertelsen, Paola Piccini, David Brooks, Jorgen Alving, and Hans Lou. "Increased Dopamine Tone during Meditation- Induced Change of Consciousness." Cognitive Brain Research 13, no. 2 (April 2002)

Kölmel HW. 1985. Complex visual hallucinations in the hemianopic field. J Neurol Neurosurg Psychiatry.

Koenig, Harold. "Research on Religion, Spirituality, and Mental Health: A Review." Canadian Journal of Psychiatry 54, no. 5 (May 2009)

Koenig, Harold, ed. Handbook of Religion and Mental Health. San Diego, CA: Academic Press, 1998

Kraepelin E. Psychiatry: A Textbook for Students and Physicians. New York, NY: Science History Publications; 1990.

Lauglin, Charles, John McManus, and Eugene d'Aquili. Brain, Symbol, and

Experience. 2nd ed. New York: Columbia University Press, 1992

Lakoff, G. and M. Johnson (1999). Philosophy in the flesh. Basic Books: New York.

LeDoux, J. E. (1996). The emotional brain. New York: Simon & Schuster.

LeDoux, J.E. (1992), 'Emotion and the amygdala', in The Amygdala: Neurobiological Aspects of Emo- tion, Memory and Mental Dysfunction, ed J.P. Aggleton (New York: Wiley-Liss).

Levin, D.T. and Simons, D.J. (1997) Failure to detect changes to attended objects in motion pictures. Psychonomic Bulletin and Review 4, 501-6.

Levine,J. (1983) Materialism and qualia: the explanatory gap. Pacific Philosophical Quarterly 64, 354-61.

Levine,J. (2001) Purple Haze: The Puzzle of Consciousness. New York,

Oxford University Press. Levine, S. (1979) A Gradual Awakening. New York, Doubleday.

Levinson, B.W. (1965) States of awareness during general anaesthesia. British Journal of Anaesthesia 37, 544-6.

Lewicki, P., Czyzewska, M. and Hoffman, H. (1987) Unconscious acquisition of complex procedural knowledge. Journal of Experimental Psychology: Learning, Memory and Cognition 13, 523-30.

Lewicki, P., Hill, T. and Bizot, E. (1988) Acquisition of procedural knowledge about a pattern of stimuli that cannot be articulated. Cognitive Psychology 20, 24-37.

Lewicki, P., Hill, T. and Czyzewska, M. (1992) Nonconscious acquisition of information. American Psychologist 47, 796-801.

Manthey S, Schubotz RI, von Cramon DY (2003). Premotor cortex in observing erroneous action: an fMRI study. Brain Res Cogn Brain Res 15: 296–307.

Mesulam MM, Mufson EJ (1982) Insula of the old world monkey. III: Efferent cortical output and comments on function. J Comp Neurol 212: 38–52.

Naskar, Abhijit. "Homo: A Brief History of Consciousness", 2015

Naskar, Abhijit. "What is Mind?", 2016

Naskar, Abhijit. "In Search of Divinity: Journey to The Kingdom of Conscience", 2016

Naskar, Abhijit. "Love, God & Neurons: Memoir of A Scientist who found himself by getting lost", 2016

Naskar, Abhijit. "Neurons of Jesus: Mind of A Teacher, Spouse & Thinker", 2017

Naskar, Abhijit. "The Islamophobic Civilization: Voyage of Acceptance", 2017

Naskar, Abhijit. "Principia Humanitas", 2017

Naskar, Abhijit. "We Are All Black: A Treatise on Racism", 2017

Naskar, Abhijit. "Wise Mating: A Treatise on Monogamy", 2017

Naskar, Abhijit. "Illusion of Religion: A Treatise on Religious Fundamentalism", 2017

Naskar, Abhijit. "I Am The Thread: My Mission", 2017

Naskar, Abhijit. "The Bengal Tigress: A Treatise on Gender Equality", 2017

Naskar, Abhijit. "Morality Absolute", 2017

Naskar, Abhijit. "Build Bridges not Walls: In the name of Americana", 2018

Naskar, Abhijit. "Fabric of Humanity", 2018

Naskar, Abhijit. "Lives To Serve Before I Sleep", 2019

Naskar, Abhijit. "Citizens of Peace: Beyond the Savagery of Sovereignty", 2019

Naskar, Abhijit. "The Constitution of The United Peoples of Earth", 2019

Naskar, Abhijit. "Neurons Giveth, Neurons Taketh Away | Abhijit Naskar | TEDxIIMRanchi", 2019 https://www.youtube.com/watch?v=BNX-Q0ySm80

Naskar, Abhijit. "Mission Reality", 2019

Naskar, Abhijit. "Operation Justice: To Make A Society That Needs No Law", 2019

Naskar, Abhijit. "Every Generation Needs Caretakers: The Gospel of Patriotism", 2020

Newberg, Andrew, and Jeremy Iversen. "The Neural Basis of the Complex Mental Task of Meditation: Neurotransmitter and Neurochemical Considerations." Medical Hypotheses 61, no. 2 (2003).

Newberg, Andrew. "How God Changes Your Brain: An Introduction to Jewish Neurotheology", CCAR Journal: The Reform Jewish Quarterly, Winter 2016.

Newberg, Andrew, and Stephanie Newberg. "A Neuropsychological Perspective on Spiritual Development." In Handbook of Spiritual Development in Childhood and Adolescence, edited by Eugene Roehlkepartain, Pamela King, Linda Wagener, and Peter Benson. London: Sage Publications, Inc., 2005

Newberg, Andrew. "The Neurotheology Link An Intersection Between Spirituality and Health",

Alternative and Complimentary Therapies, Vol 21 No 1, February 2015.

Newberg, Andrew, Nancy Wintering, Dharma Khalsa, Hannah Roggenkamp, and Mark Waldman. "Meditation Effects on Cognitive Function and Cerebral Blood Flow in Subjects with Memory Loss: A Preliminary Study." Journal of Alzheimer's Disease 20, no. 2 (2010)

Nash, M. (1995), 'Glimpses of the mind', Time.

Nesse RM. Proximate and evolutionary studies of anxiety, stress and depression: synergy at the interface. Neurosci Biobehav Rev. 1999;23:895-903.

Nicolelis, Miguel. (2011) "Beyond Boundaries: The New Neuroscience of Connecting Brains with Machines--- and How It Will Change Our Lives", Times Books

O'Hara, K. and Scutt, T. (1996) There is no hard problem of consciousness. Journal of Consciousness Studies 3(4), 290-302, reprinted in J. Shear (ed.) (1997) Explaining Consciousness. Cambridge, MA, MIT Press, 69-82.

O'Regan, J.K. (1992) Solving the "real" mysteries of visual perception: the world as an outside memory. Canadian Journal of Psychology 46, 461-88.

O'Regan, J.K. and Noe, A. (2001) A sensorimotor account of vision and visual consciousness. Behavioral and Brain Sciences 24(5), 883-917.

O'Regan, J.K., Rensink, R.A. and Clark,].]. (1999) Change-blindness as a result of "mudsplashes." Nature 398, 34.

Ornstein, R.E. (1977) The Psychology of Consciousness (2nd edn). New York, Harcourt.

Ornstein, R.E. (1986) The Psychology of Consciousness (3rd edn). New York, Pehguin.

Ornstein, R.E. (1992) The Evolution of Consciousness. New York, Touchstone.

Penfield W, Faulk ME (1955) The insula: further observations on its function. Brain 78: 445– 470.

Penrose, R. (1994), Shadows of the Mind (Oxford: Oxford University Press).

Penrose, R. (1989), The Emperor's New Mind: Concerning Computers, Minds and The Laws of Physics (Oxford: Oxford University Press).

Persinger, "'I would kill in God's name' role of sex, weekly church attendance, report of a religious experience and limbic lability" Perceptual and Motor Skills 1997.

Persinger "Experimental simulation of the God experience" Neurotheology 2003.

Persinger, M. A. (1993b). Personality changes following brain injury as a grief response to the loss of sense of self: Phenomenological themes as indices of local lability and neurocognitive restructuring as psycho- therapy. Psychological Reports, 72

Persinger, Corradini, Clement, Keaney, et al "Neurotheology and its convergence with neuroquantology" NeuroQuantology 2010.

Persinger, Koren and St-Pierre "The electromagnetic induction of mystical and altered states within the laboratory" Journal of Consciousness Exploration and Research 2010.

Persinger "Case report: A prototypical spontaneous 'sensed presence' of a sentient being and concomitant electroencephalographic activity in the clinical laboratory" Neurocase 2008.

Persinger and Saroka "Potential production of Hughlings Jackson's "parasitic consciousness" by physiologically-patterned weak transcerebral magnetic fields: QEEG and source localization" Epilepsy & Behavior 28 (2013).

Persinger. "The neuropsychiatry of paranormal experiences". J Neuropsychiatry Clin Neurosci 2001.

Persinger. "Neuropsychological bases of god beliefs", New York: Praeger, 1987

Persinger. "Temporal lobe epileptic signs and correlative behaviors displayed by normal populations", Journal of General Psychology, 1986

Perry BD, Pollard R. Homeostasis, stress, trauma, and adaptation. A neurodevelopmental view of childhood trauma. Child Adolesc Psychiatr Clin N Am. 1998;7:33.

Paré, D. & Llinás, R. (1995), 'Conscious and preconscious processes as seen from the standpoint of sleep-waking cycle neurophysiology', Neuropsychologia, 33.

P. S. de Laplace. Essai Philosophique sur les Probabilites [1814], in Academy des Sciences, Oeuvres Complotes de Laplace, Vol. 7, Gauthier-Villars, Paris (1886).

Perrett DI, Harries MH, Bevan R, Thomas S, Benson PJ, Mistlin AJ, Chitty AJ, Hietanen JK, Ortega JE (1989) Frameworks of analysis for the neural representation of animate objects and actions. J Exp Bio 146: 87–113.

Phillips ML, Young AW, Senior C, Brammer M, Andrew C, Calder AJ, Bullmore ET, Perrett DI, Rowland D, Williams SC, Gray JA, David AS (1997)

A specific neural substrate for perceiving facial expressions of disgust. Nature 389: 495–498.

Phillips ML, Young AW, Scott SK, Calder AJ, Andrew C, Giampietro V, Williams SC, Bullmore ET, Brammer M, Gray JA (1998) Neural responses to facial and vocal expressions of fear and disgust. Proc R Soc Lond B Biol Sci 265: 1809–1817.

Puce A, Perrett D (2003) Electrophysiological and brain imaging of biological motion. Philosoph Trans Royal Soc Lond, Series B, 358: 435–445.

Ramachandran VS. Behavioral and magnetoencephalographic correlates of plasticity in the adult human brain. Proc Natl Acad Sci USA 1993; 90: 10413–20.

Ramachandran VS. Phantom limbs, neglect syndromes, repressed memories, and Freudian psychology. Int Rev Neurobiol 1994; 37: 291–333.

Ramachandran VS. Plasticity and functional recovery in neurology. Clin Med 2005; 5: 368–73.

Ramachandran VS, Hirstein W. The perception of phantom limbs. The D. O. Hebb lecture. Brain 1998; 121: 1603–30.

Ramachandran VS, Rogers-Ramachandran D, Cobb S. Touching the phantom limb. Nature 1995; 377: 489–90.

Ramachandran VS, Rogers-Ramachandran D. Phantom limbs and neural plasticity. Arch Neurol 2000; 57: 317–20.

Ramachandran VS, Rogers-Ramachandran D. It's all done with mirrors. Sci Am Mind 2007; 18: 16–9.

Ramachandran VS, Rogers-Ramachandran D. Sensations referred

to a patient's phantom arm from another subjects intact arm: perceptual correlates of mirror neurons. Med Hypotheses 2008; 70: 1233–4.

Ramachandran VS, Rogers-Ramachandran D, Stewart M. Perceptual correlates of massive cortical reorganization. Science 1992; 258: 1159–60.

Rizzolatti G, Craighero L (2004) The mirror-neuron system. Annu Rev Neurosci 27: 169–192.

Rizzolatti G, Fogassi L, Gallese V (2001) Neurophysiological mechanisms underlying the understanding and imitation of action. Nature Rev Neurosci 2:661–670.

Rock I, Victor J. Vision and touch: an experimentally created conflict between the two senses. Science 1964; 143: 594–6.

Rose´n B, Lundborg G. Training with a mirror in rehabilitation of the hand.

Scand J Plast Reconstr Surg Hand Surg 2005; 39: 104–8.

Royet JP, Plailly J, Delon-Martin C, Kareken DA, Segebarth C (2003) fMRI of emotional responses to odors: influence of hedonic valence and judgment, handedness, and gender. Neuroimage 20: 713–728.

Rozin R Haidt J and McCauley CR (2000) Disgust. In: Lewis M, Haviland-Jones JM (eds) Handbook of Emotion. 2nd Edition. Guilford Press, New York, pp 637–653.

Saxe R, Carey S, Kanwisher N (2004) Understanding other minds: linking developmental psychology and functional neuroimaging. Annu Rev Psychol 55: 87–124.

S. J. Russell and P. Norvig, Artificial intelligence: a modern approach (3rd edition): Prentice Hall, 2009.

Schienle A, Stark R, Walter B, Blecker C, Ott U, Kirsch P, Sammer G, Vaitl D

(2002) The insula is not specifically involved in disgust processing: an fMRI study. Neuroreport 13: 2023–2026.

Showers MJC, Lauer EW (1961) Somatovisceral motor patterns in the insula. J Comp Neurol 117: 107–115.

Singer T, Seymour B, O'Doherty J, Kaube H, Dolan RJ, Frith CD (2004) Empathy for pain involves the affective but not the sensory components of pain. Science 303: 1157–1162.

Smith A (1759) The theory of moral sentiments (ed. 1976). Clarendon Press, Oxford.

S. N. Bose (1924). "Plancks Gesetz und Lichtquantenhypothese". Zeitschrift für Physik. 26 (1): 178–181.

Sprengelmeyer R, Rausch M, Eysel UT, Przuntek H (1998) Neural structures associated with recognition of facial expressions of basic emotions Proc R Soc Lond B Biol Sci 265: 1927–1931.

Strafella AP, Paus T (2000) Modulation of cortical excitability during action observation: a transcranial magnetic stimulation study. NeuroReport 11: 2289–2292.

Simonsen R (2015) Eating for the future: veganism and the challenge of in vitro meat. In: Stapleton P, Byers A (Hg). Biopolitics and utopia. Palgrave Macmillan, New York (2015), S 167–190

Tanaka K (1996) Inferotemporal cortex and object vision. Ann Rev Neurosci. 19: 109–140.

Tesla N. "My Inventions", 1919

T. R. Society, "Machine learning: the power and promise of computers that learn by example," ed. The Royal Society, 2017.

Tomasello M, Call J (1997) Primate cognition. Oxford University Press, Oxford.

Tremblay C, Robert M, Pascual-Leone A, Lepore F, Nguyen DK, Carmant L, Bouthillier A, Theoret H (2004) Action observation and execution: intracranial recordings in a human subject. Neurology. 63: 937–938.

Umilta MA, Kohler E, Gallese V, Fogassi L, Fadiga L, Keysers C, Rizzolatti G (2001) "I know what you are doing": a neurophysiological study. Neuron 32: 91–101.

Von Wright G.H., (1963), Norm and Action. A Logical Inquiry, Routledge & Kegan Paul, London.

Von Wright G.H., (1976), "Determinism and the Study of Man", in Essays on Explanation and Understanding, ed. by J. Manninen and R. Tuomela, Reidel, Dordrecht.

Von Wright G.H., (1977), "What is Humanism?", The Lindlay Lecture, University of Arkansas, Lawrence, Kansas.

Von Wright G.H., (1979), "Humanism and the Humanities", in Philosophy and Grammar, ed. by S. Kanger and S. Öhman, Reidel, Dordrecht, pp. 1-16. Reprinted in von Wright (1993).

Von Wright G.H., (1980), Freedom and Determination, North-Holland Publishing Co., Amsterdam.

Von Wright G.H., (1985), Of Human Freedom, The Tanner Lectures on Human Values,

Vol. VI, ed. by S. M. McMurrin, University of Utah Press, Salt Lake City, pp. 107-70. Reprinted in von Wright (1998).

Von Wright G.H., (1993), The Tree of Knowledge and Other Essays, Brill, Leiden.

Von Wright G.H., (1997), "Progress: Fact and Fiction", in The Idea of Progress, ed. by A. Burgen et al., W. de Gruyter, Berlin, pp. 1-18.

Von Wright G.H., (1998), In the Shadow of Descartes: Essays in the Philosophy of Mind, Kluwer, Dordrecht.